Enchanting Love

Love's Encounter

Jeannine Ann

BookLeaf
Publishing

India | USA | UK

Made with ❤ on the BookLeaf Publishing Platform
www.bookleafpub.in
www.bookleafpub.com

Dedication

To a White Knight Prince who freed my heart and the Maker of the Universe who gave me back my humanity.

Preface

Love shifts our focus. We see the value within each person & the potential they have buried within them. We become someone who changes the world simply by existing in it. Love is the driving force behind the art of poetry found within these pages. It was born from a journey to find my free self, my true self, and my best self. Trauma may have inflicted a dark shadow across my soul but through love the darkness was vanquished, setting free my captive heart. May the reader find an escape into the beauty love bestows leading to an understanding of true love, self-love and love freely given!

Acknowledgements

To a White Knight Prince that rode into the recesses of my heart unexpectedly. An Angel full of the sun born from heaven above to save my soul. Freeing me from captivity the pure hearted White Knight Prince set me on an adventure to find the truest form of self. A journey leading me to the foot of the cross where I found true love and acceptance. Freedom from past pains inflicted by people's ill intentions washed away by grace unworthy of but freely given. Words were loosened to freely flow from a mind now open to beauty, love, and light to bestow upon the world the same such honor it was given.

1. Phoenix Fire Power

You glamor and shine as all your ill begotten pain is
artfully arranged in a heart masterfully crafted from the
fragmented diamonds thought to be forgotten
You brighten the room in rainbow disco coloration as
you bounce joyfully to a drum heard within by the
purity of your soul
For in all time, slow time, withstanding time, you fall
gracefully as a hurricane into the hearts of all to furthest
lands held in hand saving more than can be perceived
You shake the core as to the sky you soar in Phoenix fire
power born from the ashes meant to destroy though
tougher it built you still
A universe was born in the crystal of your eyes as the
soul you portray is born out of dark by the dawn it
imparts with explosions of a rainbow simulation
You sing a melody tender and sweet yet wild and free
dancing gracefully as a wave on the sand or a leaf in the
wind as it meets its final resting place in silent serenity
For in loving so deeply you connect time and space

every race to move in accord evermore due to the heart
observed from afar

2. Fairytale Love

Hide the feeling trap it tight for none could fathom the
depths of the darkness down within.
It overcomes consumes holding hostage the heart of
stone and wire cages within the loneliest walls of steel
One touch one glance throws the shades open as light
pours in upon the surfaces covered in dust and web
A lingering sent fills the room roaming the halls and
clearing the soot from the walls stairs everywhere
Gleaming as each new smile cracks the ever-weakening
facade of resistance attempting to bar the door as a fire
builds behind
Nothing can stop the barrage as the consuming nature of
love bursts forth from inside shattering the chains and
blasting the doors free with great force
The angelic appearance of love on the horizon pure
white marching in claiming the heart with which none
can deny its place
As the heart is filled with the glowing heat from loves
embrace none can fathom the spark of its production
Now in all its ways it can live no longer in its cage

having felt its sweet freedom yet releasing to the wind
the object of its greatest affection
Expecting all to be lost as it slips to dark and the world
grows dim around the edges as the heart clings to its
humanity
Shattered to the floor crippled by a longing too intense
for words the glitter flower withers to the sound of
deafening silence
Yet glows the ever-growing sound of love approaching to
reclaim the heart it fought so valiantly to free
As it races to the side ever more to twine the two flames
of fate together with but another glance and a kiss that
seals the deal

3. Reflecting Love

The true beauty of love flowing strong and unrelenting
from the source of happiness itself
It's a glow created from the holiest heart and purest soul
grandly placed in skies to vanquish darkness
A mighty trinity of serenity as waves on the sand
brightening day and night, night and day with its might
Its love so strong it encompasses the very meaning of the
word in its rays as it burst forth from the inner sanctum
Core over heating yet somehow calm and docile in
nature for within its clutches stands the power to
annihilate all
A catastrophic event held back by the greatness of one
with such overwhelming grace and mercy
For none could Nar comprehend the full magnitude of
such unconditional love bestowed upon a broken heart
For it heals and mends the hills and valleys engraved by
oldest days bringing an intensity to the love and
intertwining the fates of both
Loosing an arbitrary of emotion into spaces undefined
and forever etched in the recesses of both connected

cores
A strength so overpowering is formed by the connection
it leads to an envy of the moon for its majestic
placement and purpose of reflecting the light of the sun

4. Caught in the Depths

Magic and Star dust born in the sky starlight that
sparkles formed in the eye
Captured and held in laser beam track found in the spirit
lost in the act
Faltered and spinning to the depths of the deep
Pulled in the current and lost to the sea
Grip everlasting playing the game
firm as the stone strength to regain
Vibration of feeling producing a sound
Rhythmic asylum magnetic astound
Vibrant and colorful cosmic display
More than the rainbow ancient of day
Carry the longing sink in the wave
Nothing to fear power to save
Many a way to get lost in the words
When caught by the eyes with a depth such as yours

5. Hearts Love

It's there hanging within the backgrounds of the mind a longing too strong to let go of and a desire to hold this beautiful soul for all time dancing within the hollows of the heart.

It's a feeling so vast none see how it can exist when it was lit for another without the help of the other.

It is a strong inferno racing out of control eradicating every other potential from the field upon its way.

None can compare to the strength of this love so deeply rooted within the fibers of the being interlaced in colored rainbow strains braided intricately into all parts of the fire heart.

What more can one do once this sensation has found purchase in the unsuspecting chasms of the cavernous city within.

For none could deny or release such a formidable presence it has produced and procured a warmth that embraces the heart in a cocoon to tight and safe to ever walk away from.

For in its place, it would leave a black hole

uncontrollably broken in its wake that nothing can repair in its absence.

6. Captivated

It lights up the night in beauty and splendor as people
give pause to see it explode into brilliant light reigning
down upon the land in a standing ovation of glittered
stars
it's an overflow of feeling spanning the farthest galaxies
ringing through the ages as timeless as life itself
breathing in harmony with the waves and wind
It's a current of air lifting the heart to soar through the
sky shaking hands with the clouds as it reflects the sun
in a perfect rainbow
It's a torrent of color dancing on the
mind lighting the imagination lost within a whirlwind of
the greatest montage of glitter glass captivating the eyes
None can nary look away for it draws the full attention
tracing a silhouette through the planes of life striking a
match to burn every fragment of pain in its wake
It's a raging inferno that builds in anticipation of its
fabled lover unsure when and where to expect such a
longing to be understood
For nothing can come close to the infinite vastness it

produces as the stroke of midnight brings to life the
desire and hope once believed forgotten
Now as it's seen in techno music vibrating through the
sands of time to ricochet off every corner and byway to
the depths of longing intensity
Once set free from the gaze the meddled mind spinning
and spiraling lands on a blanket of down unable to move
as eyes slowly flutter lost to it evermore

7. Leap of Faith

Standing on a precipice trying to keep my faith staring
into the way ahead as I try to fight the pain
Behind is all the enemies that have pursued me to this
place they stare and wait anticipate glee upon their face
I hear the Lord whisper trust and take a leap dare I
believe these mangled wings can glide and fly for me
I hold my breath and take a step and leap into the abyss
for in the Lords arms I am kept knowing he never lets
me miss
As I try to hold my butterfly wings open to the wind, I
realize the biggest lie is thinking I can't fly
For though I'm feeble when alone spinning out of
control with him I'm strong and sturdy he won't let me
fall
Failing is a mindset between success and defeat for in his
arms I'm kept he always rescues me
Days are hard and life a mess but with the lord I can find
that when it's meant to happen, I can rest in the divine

8. Foundness

Because you care the broken shattered pieces of my
heart where artfully rearranged into a mosaic picture
frame
You illuminated the dark with a glow softly still guiding
me to you in the frigid night till I find my hope again
It produced a warmth inside of me that cascaded through
time to unwind in the mind as a wave of tranquil waters
A vast array of rainbow color dancing in the wind of
change blown into the core of my creation
My consciousness slowly turning to the light it so
desperately needed finding a hope, for living is different
than feeling alive
It's a product of being recognized seen and cherished to
the deepest parts of a person's inner workings feeling
seen unlike before
Upon arriving the heart already knowing what the mind
took time to comprehend this was where it would begin
For this is the feeling of home. The warmth after
uncontrollable cold. The foundness longing now fulfilled
within.

All of this the product of the beautiful glow given so
freely to the hollowed person lost in the darkened
landscape who now is forever now found by you

9. Intensity of Feeling

It's hidden somewhere deep where none can see it
except God. A well disguised ruse.
Something so strong, at times it escapes out of the eyes
and leaves a glitter trail on the cheek.
It harbors an intensity that no one can comprehend or
see. Until one day it finds purchase within this world
bursting forth in a turret of emotion too strong to
control.
It levels the field and opens the eyes to a new reality. For
its escape was unexpected, unprecedented, and
unpredictable in nature.
Forceful and strong a longing to be noticed triggering
the release after being locked in captivity for so long. It's
a lion's roar screaming in protest to its capture and
flying into the light of day after being lost in great
darkness.
The blunt nature of its departure, too much to
understand for the recipient knew not of its intensity
staring in awe of the magnitude in which it springs
forth.

Blinking into existence after growing from seemingly nowhere. For it was for them, to them, and of them, in this frame for all time.

10. My Existence

You're an integral part of my existence holding the very
essence of my life with the power to crush to powder the
very breath in my lungs two parts of one whole
You're nestled deep in my being holding tight to the
strings of my heart as a kite pulled by the wind as it
soars to the sky echoing the light of day.
You're lighting the woodwork with lines etched in the
grain spelling out a rhythm and rhyme as my heart
keeps time to your thunderous beat
Hooves to the ground such power and grace overflowing
from the gates of heaven to bestow upon us the gift of
everlasting love eternity pure and free
For nothing can hold such formative control over a free
spirit such as I than the love engrained too deep to dispel
from within its inner depths
For you're established within my existence in such an
infallible way woven into the bands of my psyche too
tight to unwind an intricate design of grandeur
Yet still may it be for none other could hold so tight to

the wild stallion heart within me than someone with
such gentle purpose as you!

11. Transcendent Love

Look upon this love arising above the tide smashing
across the sand Breaking the barrier of sound itself
Ageless and timeless it stands stronger than a mountain.
Fierce as a lion charging forward as a bull seeing red
It's a love that transcends space dancing in circles across
the surface of the heart to show its unwavering devotion
Unfaltering unchanging evolving instead to hold tighter
and fight harder through even the darkest of valley
No greater feeling has one than this to find themselves
hung within the stars of a transcendental heart
For transcendent love is a rare phenomenon so scarcely
seen or found that to have the chance to behold it is but
once in a lifetime
So, when such a rarity of heart finds its way to its
interstellar companion to form a bond so pure and
cataclysmic may nothing tear asunder

12. Forever Bound

These hearts are pulled together with a great magnetic force lending two wayward souls to life drifting never more
An anchor to the darkness where they drifted all alone now to the other tied there is a happiness so strong
Gravity pulls in gently and anchors to the spot a force slowly growing strong the two forever caught
Destined to meet though out of reach the universe cries loud. See two hearts so drawn by love will together be love bound
It's a force so strong nothing can stop for it spans all time and space for all can see and knows it was always meant to be
The world can see its purpose and wills it to exist for the love of hearts as strong as these will forever manifest

13. Loves Flight

Softest heart held with softest hands fragile but safe in
the light held within
Pillow of grace is lent to each day by the deepest of
feeling in heart where it lay
Bursting forth as a rainbow to flight on the wings of the
clouds in the breast of the sky
Shining shimmering glitter display rivers of glory
throughout everyday
Lightening shock to restart the heart when it stutters and
falters lost in the dark
Recapture adventure dance in the sky on wings to mount
love reborn taken flight
Freedom is found glory behold a heart such as this made
to be bold
Masterly formed by the Lord of the world to lend out
love to the lost and forlorn
Happiest feelings brought to light overwhelmingly giddy
a glorious sight
So true is the love found in the hollow of wing hear
hallelujah as Angels sing

For when it does come to the start of the land may it
capture the heart and heal every man

14. Realm of the Unknown

In the dead of night, you come. Though I expect it not for
who could see in their wildest imagination something
such as this
No, for this is too unexpected catapulting a person into
the realm of the unknown making the thoughts go wild,
no explanations, no concept of time
It expands grows wild and free uncontainable ever-
changing morphing into something so intricate and
beautiful, the eyes struggle to behold it to its full
potential
What shalt someone call something so lovely woven
from the costliest of strands, tying together what none
can tear apart
So bold, so beautiful yet, so delicate one fears that they
could break it with just one touch.
Still, upon looking one can see that the sheer magnitude
of its presence proves its might that can outdo even the
strongest force placed upon it
It's the ancient of days yet also the newness of life a
sunrise yet also a sunset for it is reborn every day

something new something grand something bold.
With the capacity to grow beyond belief stronger, still
ever-changing, ever growing, ever greater more
So when you come so unexpected out of nowhere like
fireworks in the night, glittering sparkling raining down
in rainbow light
Taking it in when hue at a time basking in its presence,
for it, changes the heart, bidding it rise and greet the
dawn of which was made when it sprung into life
A world so vast wide open something that is sure to last
all time for time and in all time through all
All this though it was something unexpected and
unforeseeable even in wildest dreams, yet still you come
as the heart embraces your arrival

15. Loves Hug

It's an overwhelming feeling of warmth and love that
cascades over the body in waves sending serenity and
peace to every corner of the body
It overcomes all darkness vanquishing the tight knit hold
the tentacles had upon the mind and body leading to
great relaxation
For though the body started out in rigid formation
walking as if by robotic force through its everyday tasks
of mundanities it ends in thankful adoration
It envelopes all the senses pulling them into humble
accord unified for all time under tranquil skies full of
twinkling stars spread as glitter in the sky
For a galaxy sea could Nar compare to the fulfillment
given in the moments before dawn wrapped in the arms
of a love so strong it can't walk away
For any day is the best day when in the presence of love
held to the heart so close as the wings of a dove so
tender and sweet lost in a hug for all time!

16. Enchanting Magical You

Enchanting magical sparkling sun it dances around full
of laugher and fun
Spinning in wonderland tropical ice something unheard
happens tonight
Fluffy frilly panda parade jumping around in a world of
hooray
Daffodil days of strawberry lace something so whimsical
beauty displayed
Icicle castle raising up to the sky made rainbows
erupting as the light rays come by
Diamond dreams of days by the streams as the sun sinks
down a breathtaking scene
When the presence of you enters in as the dew it's light
of hope a wish coming true
Spend time with the heart as your love you impart you
form fountains of glitter wherever you are.

17. Pure Love

Clear as crystal gliding across the seas of liquid glass
dancing in the wind as grains of sand reflecting the light
as it blows past
Tranquility lending a peace and calm to the hum of busy
that fills everyday
A starlit sky at midnight fully enveloped by tender
mercy as comets shoot by
A feeling so immeasurably vast it expands the heart full
and overflowing
It explodes in all directions going beyond its realm to
affect all around
It eradicates its negativity empowered by desire to be the
updraft in wings
To send lights into the eyes of its beloved that dance
through the night as sparks thrown by fire bright
It's the strength to be more give more hold more and
love more than ever could be expected
For any heart that loves true will produce a love so pure
it will be the miracle of all time to obtain it!

18. Royal Love

Confetti in the wind sparkling in the sun, as it rains
down around swirling, moving dancing freedom of the
heart
An ever-flowing river as it ebbs and flows changing this
way and that tripping over rocks as it swiftly moves
along
Clear a path make a way for the royalist heart clothed in
blue as bright as the morning sky has entered to take its
place
A great northern star brighter than the sun sweeps in
with warmth peace and calm to provide a love so deep so
pure so sweet it beacons the hearts to believe
Oh, majesty a tapestry intricately designed throughout
time, space, and life to mark each moment of content and
pain
A woven braid of finest silk velvety soft a look so pure it
will bring tears to the eyes to behold for its mastery is
untold unlearned unknown
For its you that moves the heart the mind the soul and
leads the world to find their deepest self their happiness

lending a hand to hold in the darkest of night
You see a person and yearn for their heart doing all you
can to pull them in for your love burns stronger and
hotter than molten steel
For you know they are worthy of all the pain inflicted
upon you, too you, in you to see them smile and to pour
your love on them in all they do till the end of eternity!

19. The Power of Love

Twisting turning kaleidoscope a glittered picture beheld
deep in the heart its a rainbow of color so free and bright
more than the sum of them all
It's a free embrace held tighter and longer for fear of
letting loose lends a feeling of loss too strong to deny for
when the heart slips away it leaves an aching feeling too
deep to perceive
It's a question of sorts that sets fire to the mind filling
the body with candy colored shine bigger and brighter
than all time. More than the heart can hold but less than
it desires.
It consumes every square inch of space within a glitter
starlight backdrop of feeling that can't stop but grows in
intensity and can't fall away
A fierce unrelenting cascade of sparkling sun falling in
diamond light as it filters through the trees to greet the
scene stretched before it
The heart accepts the borage for it wishes for the feeling
to never stop as it grabs on with all its might to the
greatest power ever known

For no one can comprehend the greatness it possesses
except for a heart that has been introduced to the fire
created by the power of love.

20. Starlit Connection

As glitter in the wind catches the light of the sun as it
dances through the sky born from the throne
Extravagance found in rainbow light reflecting the rays
as the moon at night
It's a display made by nature as it shows its love to the
open hand stretch above
One heart beseeched another too drawn by the feeling it
dances through to fall upon
Grabbing releasing tension subside eyes connect into
nosedive
Interconnected two become one a feeling so strong
where'd it come from
A magnetic pull leads to harmonious dance swirled
around in hopeless romance
For in nature was born overwhelming display of love
and affection coming to play
As sunlight dropped from heavens gates to rain down as
glitter in beauty displayed

21. Lion Heart

Ice so cold it burns as fire thaws away at just one touch
shattering the walls that enveloped the lion heart
The heart that desires to love with a ferocity of a
thousand charging rhinos or a tornado hurricane
spinning recklessly
Once released it roars through the world burning as fire
through the night so bright it's seen even in space walk
to call all wanderer's home
So, clear the way and ready the path for it will send a
shockwave through time and space unlike any have
experienced
It's a love wave made to soothe the soul and mend the
broken heart into a masterful display of art with ribbons
of gold
A featherlight feeling none could comprehend rolls
across the veins producing change that never goes
unnoticed
It's a whirlwind producing everlasting newness across
the plain once so barren that now produce life in
rainbow technicolor

Showering every inch of existence in a power none have
seen but desire to hold for even but a second as it rolls
through
For once it has touched the heart and soul, they will
forever be changed producing new life there in its wake
For it shall be forever the one that is changing it all
through the fiercest of love it desires to spread as glitter
to echo through time
So, pray that none stop the lion heart from roaring a
thunderous cascade of love through the world into the
hearts in all its glory for all time